Captain Halloween

By Michael K. Spiroff

Illustration by
Heather Gorlitz

Do you know a child who loves Halloween? Do you remember that *one* haunting house where the fear was not worth the candy? Move over Great Pumpkin! Children will have fun trick-or-treating with the fearless, mysterious Captain Halloween!

Schoolchildren taunt and tease Peter "Pumpkinhead" because of his love of pumpkinseeds, which ultimately leads to a schoolyard dare: to trick-or-treat at the haunted house of the wicked witch on Halloween night. Peter never returns. For a generation, Halloween is all but banned. Until a brave schoolgirl named Clare takes the same Halloween dare Peter once took. In costume eerily similar to Peter Pumpkinhead long ago, a school-age Captain Halloween, along with a black cat named "Boo," saves both Clare and Halloween from the wicked witch, forever!

My Inspiration. My Future. My Son.

Halloween is a *happy* time of year. But a wicked witch
has the valley town of Nilbog in the grip of FEAR!

In town, there lives a young boy named Peter. Peter
is a voracious pumpkinseed eater.

He eats pumpkinseeds for breakfast, lunch, and
dinner, and in bed. The kids at school are cruel, and
nickname Peter, "Peter Pumpkinhead."

Schoolchildren dress as cowboys, superheroes, and creatures of the night. Peter wears a black cape, a black mask, and a pair of orange tights.

His fair-weather friends snicker and sneer at the costume he wears. Peter tries his best to ignore all their stares.

The games at recess turn truth or dare. Schoolmates cheat! Peter loses! The game is unfair!

Reluctantly, ruefully, Peter Pumpkinhead plays it cool. He would rather visit the wicked witch than lose the dare at school.

The witch lives in the lonely shanty on the valley top.
She lives above the Forest of Fools, where dead trees
sway and thunder pops.

The witch has a big long nose, lima bean green. Her eyes are RED, BEADY, and MEAN!

When she peers into her shattered mirror, she cackles at the sight. Her hideous smile reflects teeth ghastly green, not one of them white!

The witch hates the tricks and treats in the town down below! She loves Halloween. It's her favorite night. BUT THE CHILDREN MUST GO!

Town bells toll for trick or treat. Jack-o'-lanterns flicker up and down the street. A full moon rises. A fog appears. The night sky darkens. Daylight disappears.

Clouds creep in hauntingly. A misty rain falls spittingly. A frigid chill descends on town. Winter winds whip leaves aground.

Lightning flashes! Thunder crashes!

Halloween children gather 'round for Peter's dare at the edge of town. *Strange noises* from the Forest of Fools are the only sound.

The frightened trick-or-treaters tremble in the hands and knock at the knees. Their eyes lock on a dark forest path that winds and weaves through skeletal trees.

Slowly, somberly, Peter Pumpkinhead paces up the dark forest path. His fair-weather friends nervously snicker and run away FAST!

He spies the shadowy shape of someone among the dead forest trees. The shadowy creature belts out a LOUD GHOULISH SCREAM!

Swiftly, silently, Peter Pumpkinhead prowls to the wicked witch's house. His teeth chatter uncontrollably inside his mouth.

He tiptoes up the crooked front porch steps, one step at a time. His lips begin to quiver. *Chills* run down his spine.

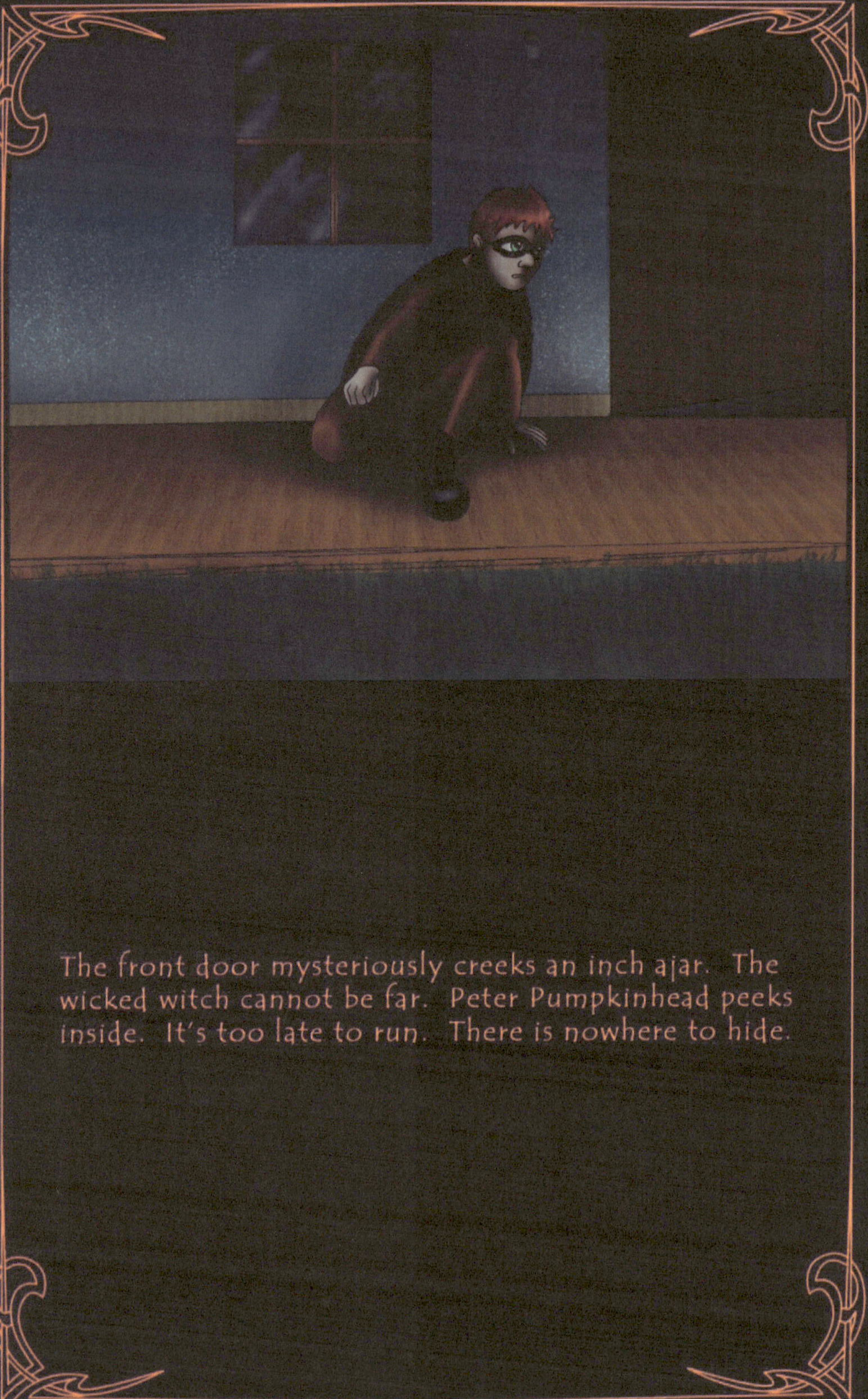

The front door mysteriously creeks an inch ajar. The wicked witch cannot be far. Peter Pumpkinhead peeks inside. It's too late to run. There is nowhere to hide.

Gently, gingerly, Peter Pumpkinhead pushes open the rickety front door. A dirty fat rat chased by a fast black cat SCAMPERS across the floor!

The rat and the cat disappear into a far back bedroom. Floating in the air, outside the open bedroom door, is a shiny-handled broom.

The house is dark but for the full moon's light.
Vampire bats, hanging from crossbeams, have Peter in
sight.

Faintly, fretfully, Peter Pumpkinhead squeaks,
"Trick…or treat." He can feel his body shaking from
his head to his feet.

He sees a shimmering shadow; he smells a simmering
stench, both coming from beyond the back bedroom.
Peter Pumpkinhead daringly decides to take a look.
He quietly walks by the floating shiny-handled
broom.

In the kitchen is a cauldron of flaming witch's brew. The thick green and black bubbling concoction smells of spoiled stew.

On the kitchen floor, Peter's eye catches something white lying next to the pot. It's a piece of lined notebook paper, in an oil-drenched spot.

Peter picks up the paper, and *shivers* at what he sees. For the top of the paper reads, "THE PETER PUMPKINHEAD RECIPES!"

He turns to run but slips and falls on the oily floor!
A "meow" and a scuffle come from behind the now
closed back bedroom door!

Peter recognizes the noise as the fast black cat and
the fat dirty rat. On his knees on the floor, Peter
ponders, "A rat cannot close a door? Neither can a
cat?"

The shiny-handled broom is gone. Peter realizes now
that he is not alone in the shanty. The town down
below hears the wild scream of the banshee.

That was the last anyone ever heard from Peter Pumpkinhead. He was all but given up for dead.

Over the town, the dark spell of the wicked witch is cast. The townspeople vote Halloween a holiday of the past.

Halloween traditions like trick or treat die. Children cry. Years go by.

Then one Halloween there comes a young girl named Clare. Clare is not afraid! She takes the Halloween dare!

Clare goes from house to house like the children of yore. She does tricks for treats at every opened door.

Parents warn Clare of what happened long ago. No one else is out for trick or treat. Clare is all alone.

A full moon lights up the chilly October sky. The town children watch Clare from their windows with wary eyes.

After visiting every house, Clare comes to a stop. A FLASH of lightning reveals the shanty on the valley top!

A misty rain begins to drizzle to the ground.
Windblown leaves whip wildly around.

Red wolves howl! Lightning flashes! Thunder pops!
Cautiously, carefully, Clare makes her way to the
hovel on the hilltop.

She feels the ghostly presence of someone among the
dead forest trees. The forest path is too dark.
Whoever it is cannot be seen.

Clare finally reaches the shanty. She knocks on the door and shouts, "Trick or treat!" in hopes of candy.

The witch inside cannot believe her ears! She asks herself, "How can this be? Children have not haunted Halloween in years!"

Her nostrils FLARE and triple in size! They are GAPING BLACK PITS beneath RED BEADY EYES!

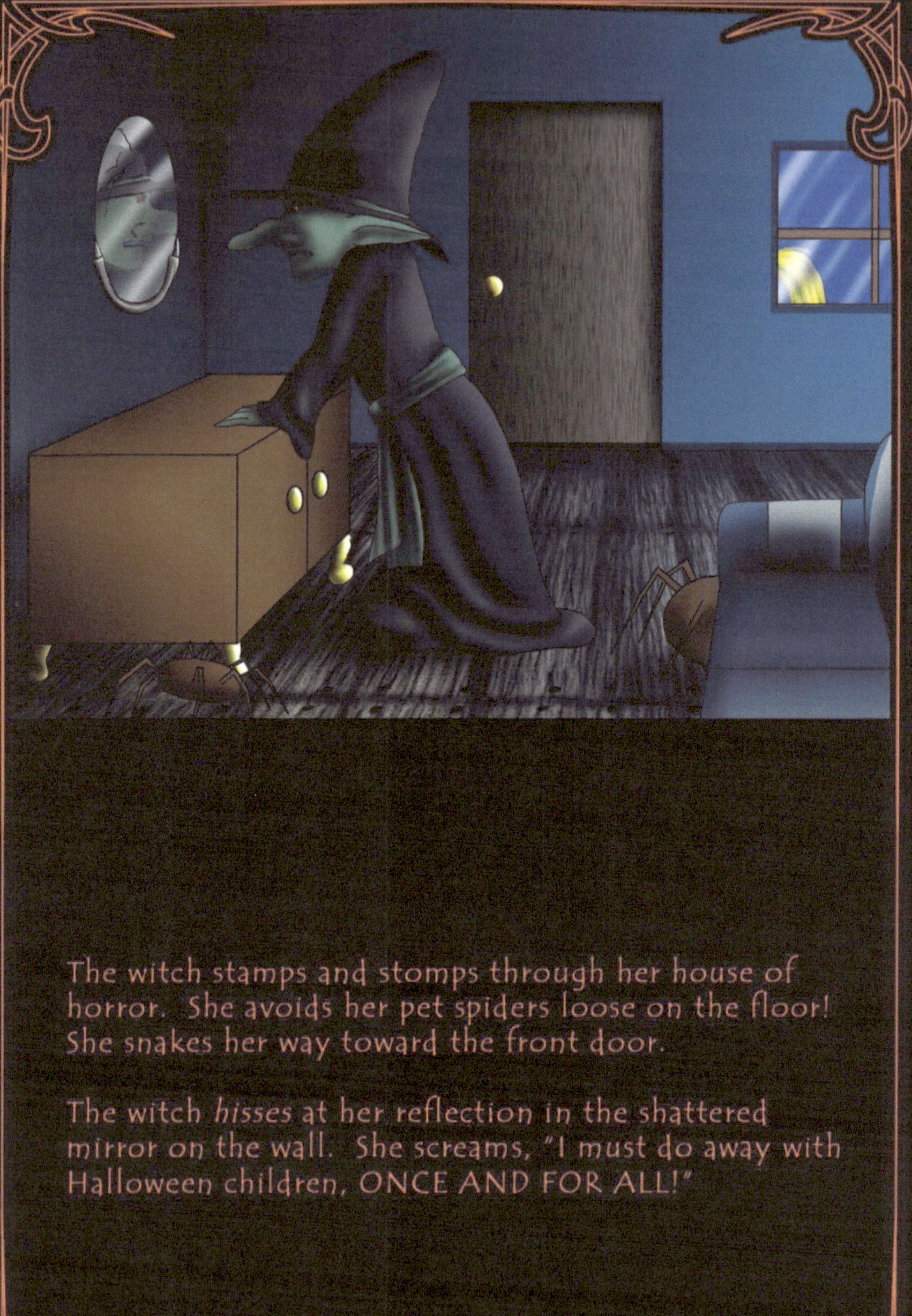

The witch stamps and stomps through her house of horror. She avoids her pet spiders loose on the floor! She snakes her way toward the front door.

The witch *hisses* at her reflection in the shattered mirror on the wall. She screams, "I must do away with Halloween children, ONCE AND FOR ALL!"

With an evil green grin, the witch wonders aloud,
"But how will I do that?" She SWINGS open the door
and sees Clare standing pat!

"Trick or treat," Clare says with a smile. The mean
green witch glares at Clare for a while.

"Trick or treat," Clare says again. A *wicked idea* pops
into the witch's pointed head just then.

The witch digs deep into her pocket, and yanks out what looks like a hairy chocolate-covered cherry. "Here! Eat this!" snipes the witch. "I made it myself. I call it a 'dingleberry.'"

The dingleberry stinks of rotten eggs, curdled milk, and spoiled meat. "Try it!" gripes the witch. "It'll knock you off your feet."

Slowly, shyly, Clare takes the dingleberry from the witch's wart-infested hands. She puts the dingleberry to her mouth, hypnotized by the witch's commands.

SUDDENLY! SURPRISINGLY! Just before Clare takes a big bite! There comes an unbelievable sight from out of the night! He wears a black cape, a black mask, and a pair of orange tights!

The orange tights beam in the night above the dark forest. He wears the letters "C" and "H" proudly on his chest.

On the back of the cape is a smiling pumpkin, bright tangerine. Above it is the word "Captain." Below it is the word "Halloween."

He sweeps in on a shiny-handled broom with a black cat he calls "Boo." The witch screams! She howls! She shrieks, "Captain Halloween, I will get you!"

The moonlight shines on his pumpkin-colored, pumpkin-shaped face. There is a sonic BOOM! Captain Halloween and Boo on the broom disappear without a trace!

A black and orange blur circles the shanty around and 'round. Captain Halloween's broom is faster than the speed of sound!

The witch cries out, "Give back my broom! Give back my cat!" Captain Halloween grabs Clare and flies away in seconds flat!

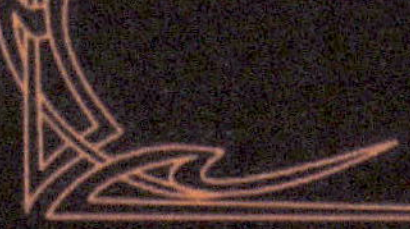

Captain Halloween, Boo, and Clare hover on the
magical broom in the air. They watch as the witch, in a
fit of rage, throws dingleberries everywhere. Flies fly
from her hair.

Captain Halloween takes the dingleberry the witch gave to Clare. He hurls it at the witch, as she RANTS and RAVES in a fit of despair!

The witch GULPS as the dingleberry lands in her mouth. She pauses, then falls to the ground with her head landing south.

She squiggles and squirms like a bug on its back! She coughs! She sneezes! She develops a hack!

Warily, woefully, the witch pulls herself up on her knees. She crawls, sickly and slowly, into the Forest of Fools, and disappears in the trees.

That was the last anyone ever saw of the wicked witch with the eyes colored red. She was all but given up for dead.

Quickly, quietly, Captain Halloween and Boo fly Clare home on the shiny-handled broom. The town of Nilbog awakes to a sonic BOOM!

Friends and family run into the street to ask Clare what she had seen! Clare tells all the town children and adults alike about the heroics of Captain Halloween!

In a gasp of relief, all the townspeople let out a sigh, for they know that Clare is not telling a lie. For that Halloween night, they, too, saw a pumpkin-shaped figure up in the sky.

Captain Halloween and Boo appear on their shiny-handled broom every October. Now children of all ages can trick-or-treat without fear, all the world over.

For Captain Halloween keeps safe every valley town! Every city! Every shopping mall! Everywhere children trick-or-treat! It's All Hallows' Eve! Jack-o'-lanterns burn brighter! Halloween candy never tasted so sweet!